The Road of Freedom:

Our Constitution's Commitment to Individuals

Edited By
John B. Miller

ANONYMOUS CONTRIBUTING AUTHORS:
Amicus
Atticus
Valerius

Published by The New Federalism LLC

ISBN 978-0-9848764-2-6
ISBN-13:
Library of Congress Control Number:

TheNewFederalism LLC

Contents

Editor's Note iv
To Our Collectivist Friends and Colleagues vi
Introduction 1
1. Economic and Political Freedom Are One American Right 3
2. Individualism...6
3. The Mountain on Which We Stand...9
4. Unpredictably Good Results..12
    The Unexpected Has Become Expected 12
    No One is Excluded...14
5. Individualism Needs Each of Us 15
    Respect the Contributions of Others to Our Own Path 15
    Tolerance for Impersonal Forces We Can't Control.......................16
    When Impersonal Forces Get Personal, Individualism Needs the
    Rule of Law!..17
6. The American System..19
    Consent..19
    Cooperation 20
    Competition..22
    Chance 24
    Collectivism Can't Compete..25
7. Bedrock: The American Rule of Law 27
    The Common Law: 99+% of the "Law" We Need.........................27
    The Stain and the Stupidity of Slavery 28
    A Correct Understanding of The Rule of Law: Durable, General
    Rules, Made In Advance, Universally Applied.....................30
8. The Positive Effects of the Rule of Law 34
    No Room for Special Interests 34
    Arbitrary Administration Is NOT Justified by Complexity..........36
    Impartiality is Required of the Government.................................38
    Poor Conduct Is Evenly Suppressed 40
    Plenty of Room for Compassion and Charity 41
9. Individual Mobility 43
    Ultimate Goals are Not Economic 43
    Mobility – In Movement, Education, Interests, and Preferences..44
    Choose Your Path! 45
10. Who Decides What Is Best? 47
11. Conclusion – America's Road of Freedom...49
Bibliography 51
Appendix A Collectivism 52
    Collectivism Defined..52
    Woodrow Wilson: American Progressivism.....................................54

Editor's Note

None of us pick our parents – chance plays a role. Mine were great. They put us first. A vacation for *them* was sending *us* to YM(W)CA camp. If we lacked for things, we didn't know it. We were busy with music, school, church, sports, friends, and each other. We taught ourselves to play golf at a course donated by Stanley Tools. A shotgun started the factory leagues at 3:30pm. Golf was for machinists.

Nor can we control our genes – that happens before we arrive. I am math-wired. I would have preferred Mickey Mantle's baseball skills. My parents let us dream. Years of school yard play taught me I wasn't Mickey Mantle. My parents advised that school, music, sports, and service were good practice to find what we liked; were good at; and what we thought we could succeed at it in competition with others. There were 2000 kids in New Britain High School. The scrum was large. We learned that every person is different, has unique interests, talents, weaknesses, and dreams. Smart, silly, foolish, honest, dishonest, good, and bad were on display each day. We all contributed to the show. We were told about it on the spot by other kids – the harshest of critics.

All of us struggle to balance family with the need and the desire to work. It is a universal challenge. None of us meet it perfectly. There is never enough time and resources. Chance intervenes. There are millions of choices how to spend limited time and money – and lots of regrets over things poorly, wrongly, or not done.

Choosing, and then *owning,* your own path is the Constitution's greatest gift. And, being free to choose is a truly wonderful gift. It is foolish to compare the *certainty* of the road we took against the *uncertainty* of the road we did not take. We cannot know the road we never took. Nor can we know how our choices will turn out on the road we choose. Chance, timing, and other people intervene.

As Americans, we have the right to explore the world about us, to learn what is known and what is not, to learn about ourselves and others, and to pursue our own preferences, talents, and interests (to the extent circumstances allow), *free from being hindered by others.*

This book is about the Constitution's unshakable commitment to *individuals,* the very core of our most important <u>single</u> right - *political and economic freedom.*

John B. Miller

To Our Collectivist Friends and Colleagues

To our collectivist friends and colleagues who cherish personal choice and individual freedom -- across Massachusetts, New England, and all of America.

This book revisits *The Road to Serfdom* - F.A. Hayek's 1944 book, seventy-five years after its original publication. Hayek's thoughts are especially valuable today.

Hayek describes the fundamental flaws in the economic and political theory of collectivism. *The Road to Serfdom* is based on Hayek's personal experience as a young academic economist in Austria, who fled from the Nazis to the London School of Economics, where he was a young colleague of John Maynard Keynes. He later was faculty at the University of Chicago, and a mentor to Milton Friedman.

The Road to Serfdom warned freedom lovers across the Western democracies about the flawed economic theories that gave Mussolini, Hitler, and Stalin political power. Hayek describes how World War II and the Cold War exposed the flaws of all forms of collectivism (socialism, communism, progressivism, totalitarianism, and fascism). *The Road to Serfdom* made the case – in 1944 – that collectivism and individual freedom cannot co-exist.

Since 1944, when *The Road to Serfdom* was first published, we have had seventy-five (75) more years of practical experience with experiments in progressive collectivism. The record is one of failure.

In sector after sector across American society, the ancient right of Americans to live freely – as they choose under the common law – has been hindered in the name of collectivist plans and programs.

Collectivism now threatens the world's most valuable asset – the spontaneous, unpredictable, creative effort of individual Americans (our human capital). It is easier to see where collectivism leads us.

The Road of Freedom is a positive statement of just a few key ideas:

- *Economic and political freedom* are ONE American right;
- *Individualism* excludes no one, and is the foundation of diversity, our economy, and generation after generation of advances in science, medicine, and technology;
- The American Rule of Law – founded upon *consent, cooperation, competition,* and *chance* – has proven over and over to be the world's best system for protecting *individual political and economic freedom:* (i) from special interests, (ii) from arbitrary government administration, and (iii) from bad actors – with impartiality, compassion, and charity.
- The defining difference between *individualism* and *collectivism* is this: In pursuit of your plans, who decides what is best – you or government?

It is time to make the positive case for getting back to basic constitutional principles – to *individualism* based on the American Rule of Law.

It is time to get back on *The Road of Freedom.*

Amicus, Atticus, Valerius

Dedicated to F.A. Hayek, on the 75th anniversary of *The Road to Serfdom.*

Introduction

We shall not grow wiser before we learn that much that we have done was very foolish. – F.A. Hayek[1]

This is NOT a book about political parties, although those who disagree with it will say so. This is NOT a book about the media, our current President, or our last President, although those who disagree with it will say so. And, this is NOT a book about sectional rivalries: South, North; East, West; Mid-West, the Plains, the Coasts, and the Rockies.

We need to be Americans again – tolerant and respectful of one another! We have substantive problems that contentious sound bites on social media won't and can't address. Normally, *tone* isn't much to worry about because we still have the legal right of free speech and the right of association. Public officials come and go. They are just *temporary* caretakers of *our* constitutional government, not *their* government. The majority of us are trying to work, raise families, mind our own business, and pay it forward to the next generation. The majority of us are just trying to live, without being unfairly hindered.

More worrisome is the *substance* of public discourse. We are beginning to wonder whether the political establishment has any idea what they are doing. Sometimes, it seems we are watching some weird football game in Washington – <u>played sideways across the field</u>. Neither team has any interest in heading for a goal line – they would rather drive at the other team's bench. The brawl has become tiresome, an unending fight about which grievance is worthy and which is not. Division, frustration, and interference with the lives of millions of Americans is the result. Instead of taking care of the playing field for all Americans, the brawlers think THEY are the show

---

[1] *The Road to Serfdom*, F.A. Hayek, supra, at p 237.

– owning the field and us.

It's time to think carefully, for ourselves and for each other – as Americans. Those who would limit individual freedom have intensified their criticism of our economy, our laws, and our form of government. We have wandered off the *Road of Freedom* over the last century, away from widespread support for *individualism*. This book makes the case that it is time to renew our ancient constitutional mutual commitment to our most important single right: *political and economic freedom.*

The first Americans died for the United States on the historic battlefield at Lexington, Massachusetts. Paul Revere's midnight ride took him there on April 18, 1775, after he saw two lanterns in Boston's Old North Church. The British were on the move, and minutemen from dozens of towns near Concord rose to stop them. Just as the Minutemen of Lexington and Concord did in 1775, Americans need to look to themselves, and to each other, to put the gibberish of factions away.

The *Road of Freedom* still sits right next to every American, if we will but read and follow the Constitution – with real respect and tolerance for each other.

Amicus, Atticus, Valerius

1. Economic and Political Freedom Are One American Right

[E]conomic freedom is . . . an indispensable means toward the achievement of political freedom. – Milton Friedman[2]

Two disconnected events in 1776, on opposite sides of the Atlantic Ocean, re-shaped Britain, created the United States, and forever changed Western Civilization.

On this side of the Atlantic, in Philadelphia, Thomas Jefferson wrote the Declaration of Independence, with its unique concept that <u>economic and political freedom are one</u>. George Washington, Benjamin Franklin, and James Madison (with others) extended this concept at the 1787 Constitutional Convention. The people of the United States put this single, combined freedom into constitutional bedrock in 1789, when the people ratified the United States Constitution in each of the states.

Separately, on the other side of the Atlantic, also in 1776, Adam Smith published the first rigorous academic work - *The Wealth of Nations* – describing how individual freedom would expand economic activity across Western Civilization. Adam Smith foresaw what the American miracle has since confirmed – *consent, cooperation, competition, and chance* would transform privileged monarchies and monopolies into societies where individuals were free to shape their own lives. F.A. Hayek described in 1944 what Adam Smith predicted in 1776:

[This] transformation . . ., where man gained the opportunity of knowing and choosing between different forms of life, is closely associated with the growth of commerce. From the commercial cities of northern Italy, the new view of life spread with commerce to the west and north, through France and the southwest of Germany to the Low Countries and the British Isles, taking

---

[2] *Capitalism and Freedom*, University of Chicago Press, at pp. 7-8 (2002).

firm root where there was no despotic political power to stifle it.[3]

In these two sentences – Hayek captures the core idea of America. Each of us has the opportunity to learn and then choose among different paths in life. Each of our choices, combined with one another, creates a powerful force for the growth of commerce. Political and economic freedom go together. They are inseparable – one – the opposite sides of the same coin. Hayek identifies the greatest danger to freedom – *political power that would stifle it.* The only force powerful enough to stifle political and economic freedom is government, and self-serving groups who seek and get the ear of government. We call them factions, but many call them "special interests." While factions trouble our society today, we have little to fear from individuals pursuing their own preferences under the American Rule of Law.

Benjamin Franklin was aware of the progress individuals were making in shaping their own lives. Franklin knew Adam Smith, and visited the British shop of James Watt – the inventor of the steam engine. The world was specializing – in agriculture, manufacturing, and transportation – wherever there was political and economic freedom to do so. Specialization has always been the driver of economic growth in the United States.[4] As fewer farmers reliably produced more and more food, other Americans were free to pursue paths outside farming.[5]

Jefferson, Washington, Franklin, Adams, Hancock, Madison – all the Founders – understood the economic opportunities of their age. They understood that *political freedom* - one side of the coin - would allow individuals to know and choose for themselves how to pursue their talents and preferences - *economic freedom* - the other side of the coin. *Political freedom* would allow individuals to produce

---

[3] *The Road to Serfdom*, F.A. Hayek, supra, at p. 69.

[4] See, for example, Michael Porter's trilogy of texts on the subject. *Competitive Strategy* (1980), *Competitive Advantage* (1985), and *The Competitive Advantage of Nations* (1990), the Free Press, a Division of McMillan, Inc. Professor Porter uses the term differentiation to describe industry specialization.

[5] In 1776, 19 of every 20 workers in American were employed in agriculture. *Free to Choose*, Milton & Rose Friedman, Avon Books, at p. xvii (1980). Less than 1 of every 100 were so employed in 2014. *U.S. Bureau of Labor Statistics*, 2015 (Table 2.1, Employment by Major Industry Sector).

spontaneous, unforeseen, advances in science, engineering, and technology – *economic freedom.* The Founders rejected the notion that politics and economics are separate and unrelated.

Over the past 100 years, legislators and parties have experimented with the very different view that individual freedom is a political issue, that material welfare is an economic issue, and they aren't connected. Nobel laureate Milton Friedman describes this divide.

> *It is widely believed that politics and economics are separate and largely unconnected; that individual freedom is a political problem and material welfare an economic problem; and that <u>any kind of political arrangements can be combined with any kind of economic arrangements.</u> . . . [My] thesis . . is that such a view is a delusion, that there is an intimate connection between economics and politics, that only certain combinations of political and economic arrangements are possible, and that in particular, a society which is socialist cannot also be democratic, in the sense of guaranteeing individual freedom.* – Milton Friedman[6] [emphasis added]

- Can <u>any</u> political arrangement be combined with <u>any</u> economic arrangement, without destroying individual freedom?
- Can political freedom exist without freedom in economic affairs?
- Can socialism and freedom be combined?
- Or, did the Founders establish durable protections in the U.S. Constitution for a single American right to both *economic and political freedom*?

Our legislators and political parties have been arguing about these issues since Woodrow Wilson's Presidency in 1912. It is time to unpack and re-state the arguments for *individualism*, for the Constitution, and for the American Rule of Law. It is time to make the broader argument that it is political factions – not our institutions – that are the source of our present troubles.

Valerius

---

[6] *Capitalism and Freedom;* University of Chicago Press, at pp. 7-8 (2002).

2. Individualism

We hold these truths to be self-evident, -- that all men are created equal; that they are endowed by their creator with certain inalienable rights; that among these are life, liberty, and the pursuit of happiness. – Thomas Jefferson[7]

Thomas Jefferson clearly understood *individualism* when he wrote the opening sentence of the Declaration of Independence. So did James Madison, Benjamin Franklin, and George Washington in 1787, when they wrote the U.S. Constitution.[8]

Individualism combines elements of ancient Greek philosophy, early Christianity, and the Renaissance. *Individualism* is a substantial component of Western Civilization. Individualists believe (i) in common respect for each individual as an individual, (ii) that each individual's views and preferences are "supreme in her own sphere", and (iii) that society benefits when each individual is free to develop his own talents as he prefers. [9]

Individualism and *diversity* are the same thing. They are not in opposition to each other! Each encourages an increasingly complex society in which the separate expertise of individuals enriches all of us and drives innovation, while individuals move through their lives with as much mobility as chance, hard work, and talent permit. The *diversity* that results – namely, trillions of different (and competing) interests, talents, and preferences among billions of people – is far beyond the ability of any human mind to hold – and light years beyond the mind's ability to fully understand.

The idea that any one of us (or a group of us) could consciously hold trillions of interests in mind, ranked in order of priority, and respond through government planning is *fiction*. It is *impossible* for any man

---

[7] Declaration of Independence, July 4, 1776,
[8] We leave the stain and the stupidity of slavery aside until Chapter 7.
[9] *The Road to Serfdom*, F.A. Hayek, supra, at p 68.

or woman to understand the prioritized list of all these interests, and then devise a collective plan that allows everyone to pursue their interests in their desired order. And, it is *preposterous* to claim that such a collective plan could be continuously revised (24-7-365) as people's interests, talents, and preferences change every day; and as new people are born, and others die.

It is *individualism*, not collective government decision making, that has driven Americans -- and therefore America -- forward since Jefferson proclaimed it in the Declaration of Independence. The solutions the Founders devised to protect *individualism* -- set forth in the United States Constitution -- were ingenious and durable.

The Declaration, the Constitution, and state constitutions confirmed inalienable political and economic rights that come with birth in the United States or naturalization. Each citizen has the right, within the law, to pursue her own talents, preferences, and values, rather than somebody else's. In his own sphere, his choices are supreme, and are not to be dictated by others. She is free to make her own choices, based on her own views, how best to pursue her interests. [10]

Individualism does not assume that people are, or ought to be, selfish about money, property, or anything else. Just the opposite! No person is entitled to be selfish at someone else's expense. And, more importantly, *individualism* relies on people treating each other well -- with respect, tolerance, and in cooperation with one another.

Individualism is what allows *diversity*, in thought, word, skill, and deed. Americans are allowed, from childhood, to explore, to test, to try, to fail, to learn, and to adjust -- and to do this again and again. Our society encourages us to try to foresee the results of our efforts, against the efforts of others, to carefully choose our own unique path through life. Without dictation by others! American kids have been free for generations to swing their elbows as long as they don't hit

---

[10] Hayek says it this way: "From this the individualist concludes that individuals should be allowed, within defined limits, to follow their own values and preferences rather than somebody else's; that within these spheres the individual's system of ends should be supreme and not subject to any dictation by others. It is this recognition of the individual as the ultimate judge of his ends, the belief that as far as possible his own views ought to govern his actions, that forms the essence of the individualist position." *The Road to Serfdom*, F.A. Hayek, supra, at p 102.

someone else on the nose.

Abraham Lincoln tied achievement to advancement — the essence of *individualism*.

The way for a young man to rise, is to improve himself every way he can, never suspecting that anybody wishes to hinder him.[11]

A capacity and taste for reading gives access to whatever has already been discovered by others. It is the key, or one of the keys, to the already solved problems. And not only so, it gives a relish and facility for successfully pursuing the yet unsolved ones.[12]

Individual responsibility is the flip side of the chance to explore, to try, and to fail. And, responsibility develops character. Character includes the obligation to learn from the results of your choices, to adjust, and move forward yet again. Character is closely related to one of *individualism's* most basic premise – common respect for each individual AS an individual. Americans are willing to take their own risks, to bear the consequences, to stand alone if necessary, and to cooperate with others for common ends.

American *individualism* assumes that in the vast majority of situations, Americans don't need to be watched to do the right thing. The moral choices we make every day – intellectual honesty, truth, respect for others, tolerance, independence – have meaning "only where we are responsible for our own interests and are free to sacrifice them."[13] There is little moral value in a decision someone else compels.

Independence of mind and strength of character are regularly found in those who gain confidence through *individualism*, because they have explored and pursued their own way in the world through their own effort. This may be *individualism's* most important contribution to our society – a spirit that knows no upper limit and that encourages ingenuity and hard work.

Atticus

---

[11] *Quotations of Abraham Lincoln*, Applewood Books, at p. 32 (2003).
[12] *Ibid*, at p. 27.
[13] *The Road to Serfdom*, F.A. Hayek, supra, at p 216.

3.   The Mountain on Which We Stand

Anything that won't sell, I don't want to invent. Its sale is proof of utility, and utility is success. – Thomas Edison

The United States is the most complex collection of individualists in world history. From a nation oriented around agriculture in 1776, individual effort has produced a society in which every worthy activity and specialty known to mankind is available. The transformation took twelve (12) generations – only 240 years!

Consider that! Today, we see modern America, with its daily diet of new software; new phones; new products; new materials; new ways of banking, communicating, and shopping; new cars; new movies; new music. The pace of change is incredible – as are the choices available to us in how we understand, and then choose, our way to work, play, and live. This generation is in the computer age and at the beginning of what may become the genetics age. But, it is just one of a dozen similar American ages of innovation, growth, and change.

Every American generation has experienced the same wonderment. Just the content and the speed of innovation changes.

The same incremental process built the most complex society in the history of the world – brick by brick, book by book, idea by idea. Here are a few examples, just a small fraction of the effort of twelve generations to build America's complex economy and individualist society.

It wasn't until the early 1800s that the steam engine came into practical use. Steam was deployed in thousands of settings by ingenious Americans – creating many more thousands of new businesses, and extending the reach and productivity of farms through better transportation. The horse and the strength of the human back were slowly replaced by machines that could move people and things. Travel times were cut, people and goods could move from the Mid-West to Eastern markets, and settlers and their belongings could move in the opposite direction. As farm productivity grew alongside transportation, more Americans were free to pursue opportunity as they thought best, fashioning new paths for themselves, their families, and indirectly, for fellow citizens.

In the 1870's, the mass production of steel wire allowed John Roebling to design and build the Brooklyn Bridge. Mass production of Bessemer steel got railroads over the Mississippi. Steel created yet another massive diversification in products. The nation built up, out, under, and across the continent. Skyscrapers, tunnels, bridges, elevated railroads, rail, and shipping are examples. But, cars, trucks, cranes, large equipment followed. New engineering disciplines formed at universities across America to more effectively use steel. Steel was incorporated into transportation networks, which improved again, along with communications, extending the reach of farms. Improvements in concrete followed. The introduction of reinforced concrete (with steel inside) followed, extending the design and construction of long span bridges and large buildings.

Thomas Edison's practical incandescent light bulb in 1879, after thousands of failed prototypes, helped to launch yet another American age – one reliant upon electricity, its generation, transmission and distribution, engineering, and millions of products, materials, companies, investors, and employees. Edison also invented the phonograph and the motion picture – contributions that led to new paths for millions of Americans to consider in entertainment – the very existence of Hollywood.

The gasoline and diesel engines produced similar ages of economic change in America. Henry Ford's Model T, in 1908, was the first car produced on an assembly line for sale to the general public. Numerous prototypes preceded the Model T. By 1928, more than 15 million Model T's were produced. Powered by a gas combustion engine, it could burn gas, kerosene, or ethanol. As the auto industry grew, thousands of products, suppliers, companies, investors, and employees fashioned new paths for individuals, their families, and fellow Americans.

Over twelve generations, transportation modes for typical American families changed from foot, sail, horse, and wagon to rail, automobile, and the airplane. Modes of communication changed from a postal service on horseback to the telegraph, telephone, radio, email, the web, and the smart phone.

The list is endless – electric generators, radio, TV, rockets, the jet engine, the computer, modern medicine, biology, antibiotics, vaccines, genetics, the internet, professional sports, recreational sports. At each moment in this history, individual Americans were allowed to see and explore the world as it then existed. And, because of past and current efforts of other Americans, each of us remains free today to foresee our own path forward, based on our own preferences, talents, and interests.

All of it is owed to *individualism* – the right of each American to explore his own talents in the way and in the order that opportunity presents. For twelve (12) generations, each American has built the American economy – the buildings, structures, facilities, machines, products, and devices that past generations used and this generation enjoys.

Government didn't build the world's most complicated economy. The suggestion that government could imagine and direct the individual efforts that produced our economy is laughable![14]

Nor did Government build the world in which we live. Americans built America! Doing so has been a spontaneous and unpredictable activity since 1776!

Atticus

---

[14]"It is no exaggeration to say that if we had had to rely on conscious central planning for the growth of our industrial system, it would never have reached the degree of differentiation, complexity, and flexibility it has attained." *The Road to Serfdom*, F.A. Hayek, supra, at p. 96.

4. Unpredictably Good Results

A genius is often merely a talented person who has done all of his or her homework. – Thomas Edison

The Unexpected Has Become Expected

Excellence does not begin in Washington. – Ronald Reagan[15]

In the 230 years since the Constitution, millions of Americans with political and economic freedom generated an explosive expansion in specialization. Americans created a highly complex economy, fueled by historic advances in science and in materials, modern engineering, genetics, medicine, communications, computing, the internet, manufacturing, and controls.[16]   Even in the "old" fields of agriculture, mining, construction, manufacturing, utilities, transportation, and information, practices are so specialized and productive that less than 9% of working Americans put a roof over, feed, and clothe the entire country.[17]

All of this was unpredictable. The particulars were not foreseen – nor could they be. The order of events was not predicted – nor could they be. None of this was planned by government – nor could it be. Neither the details, direction, nor the pace of the growth in

---

15 *Wit and Wisdom of the American Presidents*, supra, at p. 68.
16 We leave the stain and stupidity of slavery aside until Ch. 7.
17 *Bureau of Labor Statistics*, 2015 (Table 2.1, Employment by Major Industry Sector). "Core" are the industries for which the BLS has kept statistics. The population of the United States at the beginning of 2015 was approximately 318,855,000. **http://www.census.gov/popclock/** Percentages are of the entire population. The data illustrates how far the lives of many Americans have come from individual responsibility for producing one's own food, shelter, and clothing. Much of these products are now produced offshore, which is another issue.

knowledge was foreseen or planned – nor could they be.[18]

But, the good consequences of specialization are now "expected", even if they are not predictable. New opportunities are "expected" from the unexpected nature of political and economic freedom in America.

The telephone is one example, from an unending list. Invention of the telephone spurred an industry to construct and maintain a national network. The emergence of cable, VOIP, and the smart phone require ongoing changes to the industry, its supply chain, and continuous re-construction of an evolving national network. Bluetooth and "wifi" technologies are changing the industry again, its network, its companies, and its products, with millions of opportunities for Americans to explore. [19]

The snow gun is another example. Jefferson could not possibly imagine that snow guns would allow future Americans to strap one or two boards to their feet and slide down snow covered slopes. The idea would have been laughable to the Founders. Yet, snow making, lifts, skis and boots, and ski clothing allow Americans to be carted up a hill so they can slide down. One more example of the unexpected and the unpredictable in our economy! It's possible because individuals are free to pursue their interests, talents, and preferences in the way they choose.

Medicine, biology, pharmaceuticals, and genetics are other examples

---

[18] Franklin, one of the great scientists of his time, knew it was a waste of time to plan for the growth of knowledge, or for progress in general. Franklin would agree with Hayek's views on this subject. *"To 'plan' or 'organize' the growth of mind, or . . . progress in general, is a contradiction in terms. . . . The tragedy of collectivist thought is that, while it starts out to make reason supreme, it ends by destroying reason because it misconceives the process on which the growth of reason depends." The Road to Serfdom,* supra, at pp 179-80.

[19] Editor's Note. In my own field of infrastructure delivery and finance, individual innovation has driven results since 1789. Individuals solved pressing problems in materials, engineering, manufacturing, and finance. John B. Miller, *Principles of Public and Private Infrastructure Delivery,* MIT, 2000, Kluwer Academic Publishers, Chapter 3. Innovation got people, machines, and goods over, under, and through physical barriers, attacked the deadly scourge of cholera and malaria, and increased the value of GDP in countries like the United States by a factor of 464 between 1820 and 1992. See, Angus Maddison, *The World Economy in the 20th Century,* OECD, 1989.

of the "unexpected" becoming the "expected" in America. No one knows what these fields will look like in 20 years, what diseases will be cured, what medical problems avoided. We don't know how future advances will affect the nature and cost of medical care. We don't know if the next vaccine or genetic treatment is just around the corner to cure or prevent disease.

While those with the talent and interest to push the frontier of medicine do so, other Americans remain free to choose differently – to chase their own talents, preferences, and interests. But, all of us are rooting for advances in medicine, biology, materials, technology, and communications that improve quality of life in the United States. Americans root for each other. We expect the unexpected.

No One is Excluded

What I'd really like to do is go down in history as the President who made Americans believe in themselves again. – Ronald Reagan[20]

Individualism excludes no-one, and is race and gender neutral. Each American is free to pursue our own preferences and interests, to the extent our talent, hard work, and chance allow. The outcome of our choices is neither known nor guaranteed. The right to make our own choices is independent of gender, race, height, looks, age, and weight.

Individualism is also independent of personal traits – the quiet, the shy, the math nerd, the un-athletic are not excluded from exploring, testing, trying, and chasing their own preferences, interests, and talents. Every young, unproven, artist, musician, singer, or athlete faces their own unique challenges, risks, and rewards as they explore and settle on their path in life.

Individualism counts on each of us to show respect and tolerance for the talents, preferences, and interests of others, just as it requires others to show similar respect and tolerance in return. *Individualism* needs each of us.

Valerius

---

[20] *Wit and Wisdom of the American Presidents*, supra, at p. 69.

5.   Individualism Needs Each of Us

Nobody ever drowned in his own sweat! – Ann Landers

Individualism cannot exist without tolerance by each individual for the preferences and interests of others. Each of us has access to the expertise of others – this makes our specialized economy work. A heart surgeon has access to an electrician – special expertise the heart surgeon doesn't have. The electrician has access to the heart surgeon – expertise the electrician doesn't have. This is a principal benefit of *individualism*, true for all of us – masons, laborers, plumbers, steel workers, carpenters, machinists, farmers, cattlemen, programmers, technicians, teachers, students, pilots, authors, flight attendants. We all depend on one another to pursue our talents, preferences, and interests, on the one hand, while eating, sleeping, working – living – on the other.

But, *individualism* is not an automatic pilot. It is not an "invisible hand" as some have claimed. Individualism can be squandered through inadvertence, intolerance, and neglect. For *individualism* to thrive in the United States: (i) we have to respect the contributions of others that allow us to pursue our interests; (ii) we must submit to impersonal forces that we cannot fully understand or control; and (iii) we need the Rule of Law, carefully structured, with universal, impartial application.

Respect the Contributions of Others to Our Own Path

It is weakness rather than wickedness which renders men unfit to be trusted with unlimited power. – John Adams.[21]

---

[21] *Wit and Wisdom of the American Presidents*, supra, at p. 4.

As specialization becomes more complex, we lose touch with the diverse contributions of other Americans. We don't fully understand these contributions. But the special contributions of others allow each of us to pursue our own path in the economy. There is no fault in this. Each of us can't know how others contribute. It is not possible for any one of us to hold the expertise of all Americans in our head.

The experienced electrician doesn't really know the path the experienced heart surgeon took to acquire her skills – and vice versa. Changes in heart surgery is the surgeon's domain, not the electrician's – and vice versa. We are consumers of the expertise of others. We can't know the supply chain that puts fruit on a shelf in a food store, shirts on a rack, or a computer in a house. But, as we lose touch with the contributions of others – we should not forget the respect, support, and tolerance each of us owes fellow Americans. Mutual respect, support, and tolerance for one another are essential components of the benefits we all seek through *individualism*.

Tolerance for Impersonal Forces We Can't Control

Never go out to meet trouble. If you will just sit still, nine cases out of ten, someone will intercept it before it reaches you. Calvin Coolidge[22]

One consequence of losing touch is that we are increasingly subject to *impersonal* forces over which we have little or no control. This, too, is no one's fault. If I choose not to grow my own food, I must find food elsewhere. I must submit to those who produce it, decide what is grown, where and when it is available, and at what price.

Usually, this is benign enough. *Impersonal* forces are often beyond any person's control. The cost of beef goes up because of unusual weather out West. A store is temporarily out of stock because a bridge washes out on the New York Thruway.

But, sometimes, these impersonal forces are within human control – but just not within our control. A store no longer carries a product line I like. Gasoline prices go up and down because OPEC changes

---

22 *Wit and Wisdom of the American Presidents*, supra, at p. 47.

its production quantity. I cannot do anything about it.

These impersonal forces can be annoying. Microsoft upgrades its Office platform and discontinues technical support for prior versions. The practical reality is that, eventually, I must upgrade or stop using my computer.[23] Airlines alter baggage policies and change fee policies. The choice: submit or don't fly. We submit gladly when it benefits us, and grudgingly, when the cost seems high.

When Impersonal Forces Get Personal, Individualism Needs the Rule of Law!

[A] state monopoly is always a state protected monopoly -- protected against both potential competition and effective criticism. F.A. Hayek [24]

I may dislike waiting on the phone for tech support or be frustrated when a store is "out" of stock, but these inconveniences are not targeted at me – they are *impersonal*. Everyone is affected in the same way. When it's personal, when we are asked to submit to forces that unfairly target us, this is a different matter. Submitting to personal decisions of others that target us as individuals is entirely objectionable.

Fraud and deception in the economy, monopoly, price-fixing, bid-rigging, denial of access to the economy, collusion, and unfair competition are inconsistent with the *political and economic freedom* at the core of *individualism*. Freedom needs constant protection through the American Rule of Law. Unfair competition conflicts with American *individualism*. Our constitutions authorize legislatures to suppress unfair competition, but do not allow them to impose it.[25]

---

[23] By choosing to purchase a PC, I submit to Microsoft's operating system, its update schedule, its compatibility with other software, and its support network – none of which I can control. This is not a new problem. Hayek predicted American's short temper with "tech support" in 1944, before the chip existed. *"Man has come to hate, and to revolt against, the impersonal forces to which in the past he submitted."* But, the alternative to doing so is far worse. *"[T]he only alternative to submission to the . . . is submission to an equally uncontrollable and therefore arbitrary power of other men."* The Road to Serfdom, F.A. Hayek, supra, at pp 211-212.
[24] *The Road to Serfdom*, F.A. Hayek, supra, at p 206.
[25] State supported monopolies, price-fixing, and collusion were roundly criticized

Protection from the wrongful conduct of others, including the wrongful acts of government, is for The Rule of Law, to which we turn in Chapter 7.

Amicus

---

by Jefferson in the Declaration of Independence. The Founders established the first common market in the world among the original thirteen states. Congress has power through the commerce clause to keep that market open and operating. Anti-trust laws, the Securities Act, and the Exchange Act were valid exercises of federal legislative power to prevent monopoly, price-fixing, and collusion in our economy, and to apply standards for the disclosure of information relating to the sale of securities in U.S. financial markets. We will return to this topic in the chapter on The American Rule of Law.

6. The American System

This chapter explores what we call the *American System*[26] for *Political and Economic Freedom*. Four concepts allowed twelve generations of Americans to build the country we see today – *Consent, Cooperation, Competition,* and *Chance.*

These are familiar ideas. The Founders trusted citizens to do the right thing, to bring common sense, individual morality, and fair play to interactions with fellow citizens.   Twelve generations have performed millions of their own contracts, and voluntarily complied with the common law of contracts and torts. This was accomplished without the need to be watched or managed by government.   It would be no exaggeration to say that 99.999%+ of the contractual interactions among Americans with each other have nothing to do with government. Everyday interactions among Americans are self-managed under the guidance of a common law system dating back to Magna Carta (1215).

Consent

No man is good enough to govern another man without that other's consent. – Abraham Lincoln[27]

Consent is at the heart of our constitutional republic and freedom. We consent to the applicability of the United States Constitution, state constitutions where we live and travel, and applicable laws and regulations. We consent to the applicability of state and federal criminal law. We consent to the applicability of the common law of

---

[26] This is not Henry Clay's *American System*, but a common-sense summary of American freedom.

[27] *Quotations of Abraham Lincoln*, Applewood Books, at p. 20 (2003).

contracts, with protections for all of us from fraud, deceit, mistake, and breach. We consent to the common law of negligence, and to the law of other torts like trespass, arson, battery, assault, and wrongful death.

This consent is mutual. It comes from each of us, and is given to the rest of us. It cannot be withdrawn when it suits us. We move through life with *political and economic freedom*, but under the Rule of Law.

Formal consent was given by the people of the thirteen original states when they voted in 1789 to be bound by the United States Constitution. The same process was followed in each of the remaining fifty states as they were formed. By vote, the people gave formal consent to be bound.

Cooperation

The true test of a man's character is what he does when no one is watching. – Coach John Wooden.

Cooperation is a core element of American freedom. We cooperate with one another on thousands of things every day: employer to employee, buyer to seller, client to service provider, and among strangers on the roads and in public places. We sit quietly and peaceably next to one another in a movie theatre, in a church, at a concert, and on a plane. We sort out who goes next at a four way stop. We line up for tickets ourselves. We take our turn – or try to do so. We prepare and file tax returns. We prepare revenue and expense accounts for our businesses. We apologize to one another when we've made a mistake, and we accept each other's apologies.

Americans do the right thing (most of the time) without being watched. *Political and economic freedom* relies on this. Without it, *individualism* and the Rule of Law cannot exist.

When we are sellers, each of us benefits from the knowledge we bring to transactions. When we are buyers, we pay for the benefits received. As kids, we watch and we learn how parents, relatives, and strangers cooperate with each other in all kinds of situations – as buyers, sellers, consumers, manufacturers, mechanics, electricians, and builders. We learn how *cooperation* allows us to explore, try, fail, and begin all over while we search to match our interests with our talents.

Cooperation gives us the chance to see how things turn out for others traveling similar paths. We have a bird's eye view of the experiences of friends, relatives, and strangers – with different interests, talent, and dedication. *Cooperation* allows us to foresee our own path forward – to chase that combination of interests, preferences, talents, and luck that suits us in life.

Cooperation is often taken for granted – but interaction with people of different views is an essential component of freedom. It is the "life of thought." Authors, researchers, and inventors, in particular, but all of us rely on interactions with people of different views in every aspect of life. Cooperative interaction is how all of us move through life.

> *This interaction of individuals, possessing different knowledge and different views, is what constitutes the life of thought. The growth of reason is a social process based on the existence of such differences. . . . It[s] results cannot be predicted . . we cannot know which views will assist this growth and which will not.[28]*

But, *cooperation* contributes much more! Interactions with others promote individual character and responsibility – to one's self and to others. In this sense, *cooperation* is the foundation for individual morality. *Cooperation* is the platform on which character, ethics, and morality is built in America.

> *Responsibility, not to a superior, but to one's conscience, the awareness of a duty not exacted by compulsion, the necessity to decide which of the things one values are to be sacrificed to others, and to bear the consequences of one's own decisions, are the very essence of any morals which deserve the name.[29]*

---

[28] *The Road to Serfdom*, supra, at p 179.
[29] *Ibid*, at p 211.

Competition

I find out what the world needs. Then I go ahead and try to invent it. –
Thomas Edison

Competition is a third core element of American freedom – in subtle
but powerful ways. We mean the kind of benign *competition* which
we all experience daily in our interactions with each other, from
childhood through old age. We learn in a grade school art class – a
benign "competition" – that the kid sitting next to us draws well and
quickly. She has more innate talent than us. The boy sitting on the
other side of us kicks the football farther than anyone in the class. We
learn that such things are usually talent and practice related. We
learn all sorts of things about ourselves as we finish school and enter
the work force – in a benign competition with others.

Our competitive experience with others is how we learn (and relearn)
(i) what our preferences and talents are; (ii) whether those talents are
real or imagined, and (iii) how much effort those talents require to
pursue successfully. We learn from each other that different skills
come easier to some of us. Lessons and hard work can even the
scales, but not always.

Thousands of American kids think it would be great to be the next
great singer, musician, or actor: Madonna, Jimi Hendrix, George
Clooney. Competitive interactions in school, in private music or
acting lessons, or in amateur musical and acting groups provide a
reality check. There are few more humbling experiences than a dance
or music recital, an acting or an athletic tryout before your peers – in
school or on Broadway – to bring you face to face with where you
stand with your musical, athletic, or acting dreams. We are all in a
form of benign *competition* with one another. Competition provides
a reality check as each of us fashions a workable balance between our
preferences and interests and our talents and willingness to work.
Most of the lessons this competition provides are self-taught, and few
of us escape the bitter pills that reality too frequently provides.

This is no different in the pursuit of jobs, careers, professions, skills,
and hobbies, or in sports. Thousands of American kids believed it
would be great to be another Bill Russell – who won 11 NBA

championships for the Celtics. Competitive interactions on basketball courts from the yard to college provide a reality check. Self-taught! In the moment, a bitter pill – but one that has redirected thousands of kids toward other interests, other opportunities.

The *competitive* experience with others is how we learn to make millions of decisions in life. It is how we attempt to prioritize our interests with our talents, and balance them with the needs of family, income, and expense. *Competition* gives us a chance to foresee, and then decide, whether the advantages of learning a skill are sufficient to compensate for the disadvantages and risks connected to it. *Competition* in an open economy allows young individuals (especially) to assess what lies ahead along more than one path, and to organize as they think best to pursue either path. *Competition* allows young people to see what is required to succeed at an occupation, and to arrange activities as they think best to do so. Young people in the construction industry learn quickly that it takes incredible skill and attention to detail to be an effective crane operator, especially, in intense urban environments. Not every equipment operator can do it. It takes skill, long experience, and a certain mind-set to be effective. Those qualified to do so identify themselves through a benign competition within the construction industry. Young people need to see what is required to succeed, as well as the rewards of success, if they are to be able to arrange their activities to chase it.

Competition must be fair and open. Entry into occupations, trades, schools, and universities must be free from unfair restrictions. *Competition* requires an intelligently designed legal framework that keeps economic paths open, and suppresses unfair restrictions on entry. This framework requires continuous adjustment, as our economy specializes and new paths emerge. Government has a clear obligation to ensure free access to the economy. Because of this, *competition* requires the Rule of Law. *Competition* cannot exist under the arbitrary rule of men.

Most importantly, where effective competition exists or can be created, it is a much better way of guiding individual decisions and efforts than central planning by government. The Founders fully adopted the 18th century liberal view to use "*the forces of competition as a means of coordinating human efforts.*"[30] *Competition* spontaneously guides human economic activity through normal interaction of individuals. It does not require conscious control by government planners. Competition "*is the only method by which our activities can be adjusted to each other without coercive or arbitrary intervention of authority.*"[31]

This is the major distinction between "individualism" and "collectivism." The argument for central planning typically begins with the assertion that our economy is so complex that central planning by government is required to reach socially just economic results. But, this just raises a different question – who can decide but the individual what is a socially just result for her. In the United Kingdom, all students take standard tests in their early teens. The results are used to separate those students who will be allowed to continue to prepare for university and those who will not. The U.K.'s streaming policy suppresses competition through a test. For students on the wrong side of a test score – the result in unjust. Suppressing *competition* has been a hallmark of collectivism for more than a century. The irony is that increased complexity in our economy does not make *competition* impossible – just the opposite – it makes central planning even more illogical.

Chance

Things turn out best for the people who make the best of the way things turn out. – John Wooden, UCLA basketball coach.

Chance is the fourth core element of American freedom. Merriam Webster defines *chance* this way: "*something that happens unpredictably without discernible human intention or observable cause. Which cards you are dealt is simply a matter of chance.*"[32]

We don't control everything – who we sit next to on a plane or who we meet at a party. We don't control whether other drivers are sober, texting, or paying attention. *Chance* makes life unpredictable. An icy

---

[30] *The Road to Serfdom*, supra, at p 85.
[31] *Ibid*, at p 86.
[32] https://www.merriam-webster.com/dictionary/chance

spot on the road! A change in wind direction! A lottery win! Our genes sometimes help – and sometimes hurt. The right doctor may be at the emergency room when we get there – or not! Bad things happen to good people. And, lucky breaks go to people who haven't worked for them.

We learn through our experiences with others that thinking ahead is the only effective way to manage *chance*. Preparation allows each of us to seize opportunities that *chance* brings them. Police officers, firemen, EMS, and military personnel know the value of preparation – it allows them to survive. Dumb luck exists. All of us know that sometimes, rewards are not always passed out on the basis of merit. And, sometimes, penalties go to those who don't deserve them.

Chance is an uncontrollable factor in our lives – part of *political and economic freedom.*

Collectivism Can't Compete

I have been told I was on the road to hell, but I had no idea it was just a mile down the road with a dome on it. – Abraham Lincoln.[33]

Government simply cannot duplicate the variety, spontaneity, or creativity of millions of Americans, voluntarily cooperating and competing among themselves in the evaluation and pursuit of their individual preferences. No person, and certainly no government, can efficiently process the billions of choices Americans make every day. Compared to individuals choosing for themselves, government planning is plain clumsy. It doesn't matter whether bureaucrats have good intentions[34] or not.[35] That is NOT the issue. It doesn't matter whether planners are smart, wise, corrupt or not. That is NOT the issue. Compared to individual choice – collectivism simply can't compete.

Before we travel further down the collectivist road we've flirted with for a century, we should ask whether the road leads to a spot we like.

---

[33] *Wit and Wisdom of the American Presidents*, supra, at p. 25.
[34] Woodrow Wilson, for example. Few doubt the sincerity of his progressive beliefs.
[35] Adolf Hitler, Josef Stalin, Pol Pot are three universally condemned collectivists.

More than a century ago, Woodrow Wilson advanced the "progressive" theory of administration by federal experts (his vision of collectivism). These were the untried views of an Ivy League professor. We now have 100 years' experience with these ideas.

Collectivist central planning has changed from the benign professionalism originally advocated by Wilson. Today's collectivists seek huge, "comprehensive", "national" legislative and regulatory "solutions" to reach undefined ends through means that suppress individual freedom. Wilson knew that planning and *competition* could only be combined by planning **for** *competition*. Today's collectivists openly plan **against** *competition* – openly seeking to suppress it. The result has been as Hayek predicted in 1944, a syndicate-like collection of large industries in which *"competition is more or less suppressed but planning is left in the hands of the independent monopolies of the separate industries."*[36] Today's collectivist legislators support massive government administration of increasingly monopolized industries. Special interests (factions) flock to DC, compete in their own separate game with opposing factions. Individual citizens are ignored. Hayek predicted this 75 years ago in *The Road to Serfdom*.

Wilson was wrong. Collectivist central planning and administration puts unacceptable restraints on individual choice. It cannot coexist with *political and economic freedom*. Bureaucrats can NEVER replace the spontaneity and unexpected achievements of individuals, pursuing their own interests, preferences, and talents, to the extent hard work and chance allow. The only mechanism ever established for achieving *political and economic freedom* is *Consent, Cooperation, Competition and Chance,* in an open economy, and under the *Rule of Law*.

Amicus

---

[36] *The Road to Serfdom*, supra, at p 89.

7. Bedrock: The American Rule of Law

Your Liberty To Swing Your Fist Ends Just Where My Nose Begins – Uncertain attribution.

The Founders understood the practical problems created when government gives men power to "administer" over other men. Men aren't angels, as James Madison pointed out in the Federalist Papers. While relatively easy for government to control its citizens, by force if necessary, it would be very hard to oblige government to control itself. Madison described this as "the great difficulty" facing our republic.

Madison's was right to be concerned. Madison wrote the Constitution in a way to oblige our government to control itself. The Founders limited the new government by defining its powers through a written constitution; by confirming that 600 years of the common law applied; and by separating these powers from the powers of the individual states. This combination is the American Rule of Law.

The Common Law: 99+% of the "Law" We Need

The life of the [common] law is not logic, but experience. – Oliver Wendell Holmes[37]

Fortunately for us, English barons put King John up against a tree in 1215, and asked rather impolitely if he would sign the Magna Carta: written guarantees of the rights of Englishmen. He chose to sign, rather than be deposed.

---

[37] Oliver Wendell Holmes, *The Common Law*, Harvard University Press, 1963, p. 5.

For more than 800 years, the Rule of Law in England, and now America, has included the common law as an essential, durable component. This is the law contained in the decisions of thousands of courts relating to disputes about every issue that can arise between individuals. If you can imagine it, there is a common law case where that issue was in dispute, a trial of facts was held, and a judge made a decision on the facts. All of this has been written down, catalogued, and tracked for more than eight centuries. The common law developed right alongside economic expansion in Britain and America. *Consent* was necessary, as was *cooperation*, to use courts to decide disputes and to abide by the results. 800 years of experience in resolving disputes produced great specificity. The common law is predictable. Parties know how their dispute will be decided based on the results of earlier, similar disputes. Under the common law, parties can foresee the likely result. This resolves disputes before the parties go to court.

The common law is about much more than contracts between individuals or merchants. Negligence had its start in the common law. So did arson, trespassing, assault, battery, wrongful death, and the common law version of larceny – "conversion." Rules of evidence come from the common law. Courts operate under common law rules. Except for statutory crimes, we run on the common law.

What would happen if (i) existing laws remained in place, and (ii) legislatures and regulatory agencies took a vacation for the next ten years? Not as much as commonly believed! The common law would be there to catch all of us – much of the entire economy! We'd learn to believe in ourselves again.

The Stain and the Stupidity of Slavery

Four passages by Abraham Lincoln confirm slavery's irreconcilable conflict with individual liberty. The freedom proclaimed by Jefferson in the Declaration and secured by Madison in the 1789 Constitution did not extend to slaves.

Those who deny freedom to others deserve it not themselves.[38]

We all declare for liberty; but in using the same word we do not all mean the same thing. With some the word liberty may mean for each man to do as he pleases with himself, and the product of his labor; while with others the same word may mean for some men to do as they please with other men, and the product of other men's labor.[39]

Familiarize yourself with the chains of bondage and you prepare your own limbs to wear them. Accustomed to trample on the rights of others, you have lost the genius of your own independence and become the fit subjects of the first cunning tyrant who rises among you.[40]

I leave you, hoping that the lamp of liberty will burn in your bosoms until there shall no longer be a doubt that all men are created free and equal.[41]

The stain of slavery in the United States is real. Slavery was much more than Madison's concern in Federalist # 51: "administration by men over other men." It was the complete suppression of *political and economic freedom* by some men over others, exempt from the laws of murder, assault, and rape – mitigated, if at all, at the whim of the slave owner.

The economic stupidity of slavery is not generally discussed. Slavery denied consent, suppressed cooperation, appropriated the labor of slaves without compensation, denied access to the economy, and eliminated chance and initiative as the source of opportunity for blacks. Slavery damaged the economy of the South, its manufacturing base, financial system, and educational system. Not only did it deny economic and political freedom to slaves, it also suppressed non-slaveholding whites across the South.[42]

---

[38] *Quotations of Abraham Lincoln*, Applewood Books, at p. 12 (2003).

[39] *Ibid*, at p. 17 (2003).

[40] *Ibid*, at p. 32 (2003).

[41] *Ibid*, at p. 32 (2003).

[42] *Battle Cry of Freedom: The Civil War Era*, by James M. McPherson, Oxford University Press (2003).

The Civil War Amendments – Amendments 13 through 15 – to the United States Constitution fixed the written version of the Rule of Law as to slavery. But, Jim Crow laws, and wrong-headed state and federal statutes, cases, and decisions failed to provide universal application of the law and open access to the economy for decades. Passed by state legislatures, Jim Crow laws were "legal", but no impartial person would assert they were consistent with the American Rule of Law.[43]

Slavery denied access to the American System of *Consent, Cooperation, Competition,* and *Chance.* The Civil War Amendments to the Constitution overturned that mistake on paper. To finally put this mistake in the rear-view mirror will require renewed commitment to the Rule of Law. Only the Rule of Law can secure the most important guarantee of political and economic freedom, whether our ancestors were slaves, immigrants, or native Americans. That guarantee comes from the individual right to control the product of our own labor – property, money, and knowledge. It comes from the individual right to pursue our own preferences, in our own way, as we choose, to the extent our talents and chance allow. *Political and economic freedom* is guaranteed under the Rule of Law. We own the product of our labor, our ideas, and our knowledge. <u>Because of this, nobody – absolutely nobody – has complete power over any of us.</u>

A Correct Understanding of The Rule of Law: Durable, General Rules, Made In Advance, Universally Applied

If men were angels, no government would be necessary. If angels were to govern men, neither external nor internal controls on government would be necessary. In framing a government which is to be administered by men over men, <u>the great difficulty lies in this: you must first enable the</u>

---

[43] One hundred and fifty (150) years after the Civil War, a few navigational aids should be added to the United States Constitution to forever fix lingering constitutional issues relating to slavery. How to preserve *political and economic freedom* for every individual in America is the subject of *The Second Bill of Rights and The New Federalist Papers*, Edited by John B. Miller, The New Federalism LLC (2012).

government to control the governed; and in the next place oblige it to control itself. -- James Madison[44]

Stripped of all bells and whistles, the American Rule of Law contains the rules under which individual American exercise _political and economic freedom_ in an open society. These are general rules, made in advance, and universally applied. Their purpose is to PROMOTE, not SUPPRESS, individual choice. The goal is an economy based on _Consent, Cooperation, Competition,_ and _Chance._ The purpose is to allow individuals to predict, with a fair degree of certainty, how the power of the state will be applied in a wide range of circumstances. Individuals need this knowledge to intelligently plan how to pursue their own interests and preferences, in conformance with a Rule of Law that binds everyone.

The most effective rules "are, or ought to be, intended to apply for long enough periods that it is impossible to know whether they will assist particular people more than others."[45] There are numerous examples. We drive on the right, the British on the left. It matters more that there be a general rule than which side is chosen. Frequent changes in the side of the road we drive would wreak havoc with car manufacturers and cause confusion and expense related to signals and road configuration.

General rules, made in advance, with longevity in mind (durable), universally applied – these are the four key elements of the Rule of Law. These allow each person to reliably foresee how the Rule of Law will affect paths he or she is considering and the choices to be made to pursue them.

For example, state law requires a particular education as a pre-requisite to take the test to become a licensed professional engineer. This requirement is public knowledge, and individuals can foresee it as they assess and adjust their path toward taking the test. This is a general rule, made in advance, made for a long period of time, and universally applied. It affects all individuals in the same way – male, female, young, old, and all ethnic and racial backgrounds.

---

[44] Madison, _The Federalist Papers 51_, at p. 322 (Mentor, 1961). References are to the 1961 Mentor ed.
[45] _The Road to Serfdom,_ supra, at p 113.

Assume, instead, that state law allows a licensing board to decide whether an individual has an "appropriate" education before being allowed to take the test. While the law may have been passed by an elected legislature and signed by a governor, such a law is not consistent with the Rule of Law. This is an essential difference – one that is currently lost on many legislators and most factions. When rules prevent an individual from reliably predicting how those rules will affect their choices and plans, the rules work against the individual because they suppress *political and economic freedom*.

> *The important question is whether the individual can foresee the action of the state and make use of this knowledge as a datum in forming his own plans, with the result that the state cannot control the use made of its machinery and that the individual knows precisely how far he will be protected against interference from others, or whether the state is in a position to frustrate individual efforts.*[46]

In our example, an individual – whether black, white, male, female, recent immigrant, young, or old – is trying to assess whether spending her money on a 2 or 4-year engineering education will guarantee access to a room controlled by the state to take a test. If the rules make this clear in advance, she can use the mechanism the rules create to plan her path with no chance of being hindered by the state. If the rules obscure the path, and make access to the test a privilege that cannot be known in advance, she can't rely on the rules to keep her path open to take the test – putting not only the path in doubt, but putting the expense of 2 or 4 years of education at risk. The first result is consistent with the Rule of Law, the second is not. That a rule is made "legal" by a legislature does not make it consistent with the American Rule of Law.[47]

---

[46] *The Road to Serfdom*, supra, at p 118.
[47] When Hayek first published *The Road to Serfdom*, Hitler had less than a year to live. The Reichstag had passed a series of statutes granting Hitler unlimited dictatorial powers, and he was using them. "It may well be that Hitler has obtained his unlimited powers in a strictly constitutional manner and that whatever he does is therefore legal in the juridical sense. But who would suggest for that reason that the Rule of Law still prevails in Germany." *The Road to Serfdom*, supra, at p 119.

Durable, general rules, made in advance, and universally applied have other advantages beyond allowing individuals to use the Rule of Law to predict and wisely plan their life, in cooperation with others. The Rule of Law creates a legal framework in which the nation's economic activity works, changes, and grows, through millions of individual choices, interactions, and decisions. This process proceeds spontaneously, without the blessing of or hindrance from government.

In this sense, the Rule of Law is the committed enemy of privilege. "It is the Rule of Law, . . . the absence of legal privileges of particular people designated by authority, which safeguards that equality before the law . . . the opposite of arbitrary government."[48]

Here is our formulation of the American Rule of Law from an earlier book. It is consistent with these principles, and written to be included in an Amendment to the United States Constitution.[49]

[1. The Rule of Law in The United States]

1. *The Rule of Law in the United States shall forever be comprised of: allocated powers among the people, the states, and the national government under this Constitution; broad liberty rights retained by the people; the police power retained by each State to preserve the common exercise of liberty rights; limited, enumerated legislative powers vested in and exercisable only by an elected Congress; separation of national powers among Congress, the Executive, and the Judiciary; and development of the common law consistent therewith by an independent state and federal judiciary.*

Valerius

---

[48] *The Road to Serfdom*, supra, at p 117.
[49] This is the first section of the first of 11 Amendments proposed to the Constitution. *The Second Bill of Rights and The New Federalist Papers*, Edited by John B. Miller, The New Federalism LLC (2012).

8.   The Positive Effects of the Rule of Law

Nearly all men can stand adversity, but if you want to test a man's character, give him power.[50] – Abraham Lincoln.

No Room for Special Interests

It is superstition to believe that there must be a majority view on everything. – F.A. Hayek[51]

There is no place for factions (special interests) in the Rule of Law. Laws and regulations that take specific aim at the needs or wants of particular people or of a group of people are not general in nature. Impartiality is required for equal justice under the Rule of Law. Laws that favor one group are just as partial as those that disfavor others. Neither is worthy of inclusion in the American Rule of Law.

For *political and economic freedom* to thrive, the Founders put mechanisms in place to prevent factions from misusing the power of government to suppress individual freedom. Ambitious men and women, they correctly feared, would seek power and influence from voters by promising to use the power of government to compel what they could not obtain through *consent, cooperation, competition, and chance.* No level of government is immune from the danger of factions. Local governments are especially vulnerable.[52]

Special interests with narrow, targeted interests have attacked the American Rule of Law since the Founding. The rise of factions

---

[50] *Quotations of Abraham Lincoln*, supra, at p. 30.
[51] *The Road to Serfdom*, F.A. Hayek, supra, at p 105.
[52] "If the law says that such a board or authority may do what it pleases, anything that board or authority does is "legal" - but its actions are certainly not consistent with the Rule of Law." *The Road to Serfdom*, supra, at p 119.

coincides with the decline of *political and economic freedom*.[53] Factions seek special privilege or favorable treatment for members. They pressure government to make rulings, regulations, or laws that the Rule of Law would otherwise deny.

Madison foresaw this in the Federalist Papers. Ambitious individuals, hungry for power and influence would be at the center of efforts by groups seeking special treatment in the administration of law by public officials. The demands would change over time, but the thirst for power would not. Before Mussolini, Lenin, and Hitler revealed their totalitarian side – progressives in America held them up as visions for central planning. Since 1945, factions have found other reasons – one crisis after another – that argue for government interference with the *political and economic freedom* of individuals.[54]

Common sense allows us to see and understand the overall purpose of these efforts – the replacement of *equal justice* for each of us <u>under</u> the Rule of Law with the pursuit of *equal results* <u>against</u> the Rule of Law. The name for this type of group-based politics doesn't matter. Nor does the source – right, left, or middle.

But, to achieve equal results for different people – government has to treat people differently.[55] And this is where collectivism falls apart. Treating people differently to make results the same makes no sense. To make two kids professional musicians – one with talent and one not – government must treat them differently. The prospects for success are dim. To make two people proficient cost estimators, one who is math wired must be treated differently than the one who is not. There is little prospect for success.

Consciously or not, factions will destroy the American Rule of Law, as Madison foresaw, unless they are suppressed through the mechanisms the Founders outlined in the Constitution, updated with

---

[53] There are special interest groups that quite properly advocate for the traditional Rule of Law – for durable, general rules, made in advance, and universally applied. These are different from the narrowly focused factions that target particular results of whatever stripe in derogation of the Rule of Law.

[54] See, 1994 Introduction by Milton Friedman to *The Road to Serfdom*, supra, at pp. 259-60.

[55] *The Road to Serfdom*, supra, at p 117,

more effective safeguards to preserve the American Rule of Law.[56]

Arbitrary Administration Is NOT Justified by Complexity

He can compress the most words into the smallest ideas of any man I ever met. – Abraham Lincoln[57]

Complexity is the excuse for massive pieces of legislation and regulation. Promises are inflated to preposterous levels before enactment. Inside these massive pieces of legislation are some of the smallest ideas in our nation's history. The results that follow are hollow, unreported, or non-existent. As our economy specializes, it is increasingly difficult to coherently use legislation to force end results. This is the failure record of factions, special interests, and collectivism. These are not failures of our Constitution nor the Rule of Law.

At the root of this cycle is a pattern of legislative "punting" that dates back one hundred years. Woodrow Wilson's academic argument for progressivism was straightforward. Because of economic and political complexity, Wilson argued, legislatures should pass statutes that give broad discretion to expert administrators. These experts would use their discretion to fashion an application of rules that fit the factual circumstances of each individual's interaction with government. This was the beginning of the regulatory state – founded on the complexity argument.

Factions falsely believe that there is a "right" answer to every question. This has never been true. There isn't even a majority view on most questions. Yet, factions spread the superstition that government's job is to impose their understanding of the majority view on individuals. Faced with increasing pressure from factions, the response from legislators has been delegation to bureaucrats – the professional expert administration that was Wilson's dream.

---

[56] See, proposed Amendments 1, 2, 3, and 4 (the Liberty Amendments) in *The Second Bill of Rights and The New Federalist Papers*, Edited by John B. Miller, The New Federalism LLC (2012).
[57] *Wit and Wisdom of the American Presidents*, supra, at p. 27.

Legislatures regularly delegate to an executive agency to conceal lack of agreement in the legislature on end goals, or to conceal the fact that instead of general rules universally applied, administrative officials will be authorized to exercise discretion on the facts of each individual case. Delegation is an admission that there isn't a majority view on an issue. This is legislative "punting," and it leads to citizens going in circles with expert bureaucrats. The "Department of Circumlocution" is what Charles Dickens called it in *Little Dorrit*. Experts you don't know, from whom permission is required.

Since Wilson's time, legislators and administrators have never managed to find the right experts, or enough experts, to get any of collectivism's major initiatives properly written, correctly implemented, with solvency. Collectivist programs have been in perpetual need of "reform," and "more money."

Discretionary application of regulations by expert officials on the facts and at the time for each individual is at odds with the Rule of Law. This is widespread interference with *political and economic freedom* – blinders put over the eyes of every individual trying to foresee what the options are for pursuing his preferences and interests. This is placing conditions on an individual's right to proceed as she chooses, and subjecting her plans to the discretion of officials. The problem is more than interference with people's ability to foresee how to respond. And, it is beyond the stagnation imposed on individuals across the economy. The real problem is arbitrary government – caused by rules that are neither durable nor general, are made on the fly, and are not of universal application. Arbitrary government is wholly inconsistent with the Rule of Law.

Arbitrary government by Britain was well known to the Founders, who wrote federal and state constitutions to require general rules, made in advance, that could be universally applied. Broad liberty rights were expressly retained by individual citizens, and the power of government was limited and allocated among citizens, the states, and the national government. States retained the police power to protect the common exercise of individual liberty rights. Limited, enumerated legislative powers were given to the Congress. National powers were separated among the Congress, the Executive, and the Judiciary. All of this rested on continued development of the common law by an independent judiciary.

Collectivists would turn this structure on its head. Factions find this appealing, because elected officials can claim to solve every problem factions advance, by delegating the solution to expert bureaucrats. In this sense, legislators and regulators have been captured by special interests and factions.[58] Elected officials cannot publicly admit that central planning of the economy can NEVER effectively replace *political and economic freedom.* But, they can pay lip service to freedom, real service to factions, raise money with their help, and support massive legislative and regulatory programs asking others – all unelected – to solve complex societal problems.

The "answers" to problems like poverty, drug abuse, lack of education, and unemployment are not even the subject of a majority opinion. It is not surprising that failure is the result when regulators "embark on a course of planning which requires more agreement than in fact exists."[59] After 100 years of failure, collectivism should be seen as the arbitrary, clumsy, ineffective suppressor of *political and economic freedom* it has proven to be.

> *The state should confine itself to establishing rules applying to general types of situations and should allow the individuals freedom in everything which depends on the circumstances of time and place, because only the individuals concerned in each instance can fully know these circumstances and adapt their actions to them.[60]*

Impartiality is Required of the Government

The most sacred of the duties of a government [is] to do equal and impartial justice to all its citizens. --Thomas Jefferson. [61]

---

[58] This why the Founders left the police power with the States. This prevented factions from descending on Washington to corrupt the federal government. The risk from factions would be diffused. See, proposed Amendments 1 (Section 4), and 4 (the Liberty Amendments) in *The Second Bill of Rights and The New Federalist Papers*, Edited by John B. Miller, The New Federalism LLC (2012).
[59] *The Road to Serfdom*, supra, at p 103-105.
[60] *Ibid*, at p 114.
[61] Thomas, Jefferson, Note in Destutt de Tracy, "Political Economy," 1816. ME 14:465.

Impartiality is the reason the Rule of Law requires durable, general rules, made in advance, and universally applied. Americans with *equal* rights want government to remain *impartial* in its dealings with us and with fellow citizens. The American government is NOT supposed to pick sides.

> *To be impartial means to have no answer to certain questions - to the kind of questions which, if we have to decide them, we decide by tossing a coin. In a world where everything was precisely foreseen, the state could hardly do anything and remain impartial.[62]*

As Americans, we want common action (legislation and regulation) to be limited to matters where people agree on common ends. For example, we agree with "Drive on the right!" As the reach of government action extends deeper and deeper into the economy, far into the affairs of individual Americans, the probability that there is common agreement on a course of action goes down – <u>way down</u>.

Collectivism is highly attractive to self-proclaimed "specialists," anxious to be given the chance to impose their love for their specialty on others.[63] There are few things more annoying than a self-proclaimed expert on a local planning board, zoning board, or commission. Governments cannot be impartial with self-proclaimed experts as decision-makers. Nor can they remain impartial when the measures taken are known in advance to affect particular people in particular ways. When legislators, bureaucrats, or planners pick sides, they substitute privilege, status, and favoritism for the Rule of Law. Government then enters political and economic interactions among individuals as a participant, one that is all powerful. It takes a side, in favor of some and against others.

> *If we want to create new opportunities open to all, to offer chances of which people can make what use they like, the precise results cannot be foreseen. General rules, genuine laws as distinguished from specific orders, must therefore be intended to operate in circumstances which cannot be foreseen in detail, and therefore, their effect on particular*

---

[62] *The Road to Serfdom*, F.A. Hayek, supra, at p 115.
[63] *Ibid*, at p 99.

ends or particular people cannot be known beforehand. It is in this sense alone that it is at all possible for the legislator to be impartial. . . . [Law] ceases to be a mere instrument to be used by the people and becomes instead an instrument used by the lawgiver upon the people and for [the lawgiver's] ends.[64]

Factions are *interested* participants in the formulation of policy, law, and regulation. They want to advance narrow, partial interests. But, Government is impartial only when the measures taken are not known in advance to affect particular people in particular ways.

Poor Conduct Is Evenly Suppressed

Of distinction by birth or badge, [Americans] had no more idea than they had of the mode of existence in the moon or planets. They had heard only that there were such, and knew that they must be wrong. – Thomas Jefferson[65]

The Rule of Law does not call for a nation of mud-wrestlers with no rules. The Founders were not fools. There ARE individuals who choose not to comply with laws, who choose to take rather than *cooperate*; who find it easier to *compete* unfairly. Some choose to use corrupt or illegal means to make their way through life. This requires "an intelligently designed and continuously updated legal framework."[66] Careful, thoughtful policy is required to support free and open competition among individuals. This intervention is the Rule of Law: durable, general rules, made in advance, and universally applied. Fraud and deception in commerce is a fertile ground for this kind of policy intervention, as it is in the sale of notes and securities (stocks and bonds). Price-fixing, bid-rigging, and other anti-competitive behavior is another area where careful government intervention is clearly necessary. When individuals choose to compete unfairly, government should take careful, decisive, steps to suppress such conduct.

[64] *The Road to Serfdom*, F.A. Hayek, supra, at p 115.
[65] Answers to de Meusnier Questions, 1786. ME 17:89
[66] *The Road to Serfdom*, F.A. Hayek, supra, at p 88.

State supported monopoly is another area where careful policy intervention is required. Jefferson wrote about suppressing monopoly in the Declaration of Independence. The Founders opposed every form of government-granted private monopoly.

But, other functions of government cannot be adequately provided by private enterprise – and are provided by government. The Army, Navy, Marines, and Air Force – are examples of government monopolies. State and local police have always been government monopolies. Other functions, like medical services, education, telecommunications, roads, bridges, transportation, water supply, wastewater treatment, and energy supply have been complicated mixes of public and private activity over the nation's history. America has seen the scope of such monopolies fluctuate, on both the public and private side. Canals, post roads, the Pony Express, streetcars, bus systems, the telephone, aqueducts, mail delivery, package delivery are examples of this fluctuation. While thoughtful laws are regularly needed in circumstances where competition cannot properly work, 240 years of experience confirms what the Constitution requires – competition should not be suppressed where it does, or can, work.

Plenty of Room for Compassion and Charity

Governments have a tendency not to solve problems, only to rearrange them. – Ronald Reagan[67]

Americans have always been a compassionate, thoughtful, caring people. Nothing in the Rule of Law, or in this book, retreats from that history or from the desirability of continuing it.

Laws providing for a comprehensive system of social insurance, for protection against catastrophic illness or physical injury are well within the bounds of the Rule of Law, applied through durable, general rules, made in advance, and applied universally.

Charity – from churches, individuals, and private organizations – has

---

[67] *Wit and Wisdom of the American Presidents,* supra, at p. 69.

always been an important mechanism for Americans to help each other. Charity is a mechanism that has unique advantages in the American System. Those who give to others do so by choice, and those who receive the help understand the source and nature of the help given.

In this sense, charity cements the connections the people of the United States have to one another – especially the connection to those in need. Individual charity is much more effective in personalizing assistance to those who need help. And, charitable connections are made free from the restrictions of impartiality imposed on government under the Rule of Law.

Valerius

9.　Individual Mobility

Pull hard and you will go fast! Peter A. Holland, MIT Rowing Coach, 1974.

Ultimate Goals are Not Economic

If you don't have time to do it right, when will you have the time to do it over? – John Wooden, UCLA Basketball Coach.

Those opposed to individual *political and economic freedom* often claim that individualists are driven by "money, money, money, money." The lyrics of the O'Jays' Motown hit confirm that "Some people got to have it; Some people really need it." But, the claim that the ultimate goal of Americans is "money" is fiction. This is just a slur that misrepresents the principles on which *individualism* is based.

Money – a pure economic end – is not the ultimate goal in any reasonable person's life. Personal satisfaction comes not from a stack of money – but from a life well led. For generations of Americans, this comes from the freedom to explore, assess, package and pursue your own path through life. No one fully succeeds. But, Americans – unique in the history of mankind – are free to form this path for themselves, and to build it through *consent, cooperation, competition,* and *chance* – under the Rule of Law. Satisfaction comes from exploring and building this path – with those combinations of family, education, work, and play that chance and effort allow.

> *If we strive for money, it is because it offers us the widest choice in enjoying the fruits of our efforts. . . . It would be much truer to say that money is one of the greatest instruments of freedom ever invented by man.*[68]

---

[68] *The Road to Serfdom*, F.A. Hayek, supra, at p 124.

The young woman who wants to be a doctor needs money for an education, not because she wants money. The young man who wants to be an electrician needs money for training, not because he wants money. Money is merely an instrument – not an end – to those who understand *individualism*.

Mobility – In Movement, Education, Interests, and Preferences

I have more respect for the fellow with a single idea who gets there than for the fellow with a thousand ideas who does nothing. – Thomas Edison

The ultimate goal of *political and economic freedom* in America is *mobility* – individual flexibility to explore, test, try, fail, and succeed in the pursuit of your own preferences and interests, to the extent that chance, talent, and hard work allow. Mobility is the principle benefit of *individualism*. Included is the opportunity to learn on your own – from a book, on-line, in a library, at work, or by experience. A quality education is essential – but the mark of such an education is the humble recognition that learning never stops and that knowledge isn't only found in a textbook.

Our constitution implements the conscious decision of the American people to confine government, in general, to the important task of creating and protecting a nation in which the knowledge, initiative, talent, and preferences of individuals have the greatest latitude under the Rule of Law. This allows individuals to plan and to pursue those plans. This allows individuals to re-set, over and over again, as circumstances, preferences, and talents change during each individual's life.

Yes, the pursuit of happiness is littered with bitter choices. Every one of us faces both joyful and bitter choices in life. None of us can avoid them in our time on earth. None of us can avoid the need to juggle what and who are important to us, what gets done, what gets deferred, and what is never done. We choose – sometimes positively, sometimes negatively, and sometimes by not choosing. Hopefully, we learn from our mistakes. Sometimes, we face bitter choices head on. Other challenges – illness, injury, death – come by chance or by surprise, and are unavoidable.

The only way to avoid bitter choices in life is to give those choices away – to put them in the hands of government to make for us. The Constitution rejected this path. If we want *mobility, political and economic freedom,* and *liberty* – transferring life's choices to government is a non-starter.

Choose Your Path!

We have progressively abandoned that freedom in economic affairs without which personal and political freedom has never existed in the past. – F.A. Hayek[69]

We are millions of legislative and regulatory pages deep into Wilson's progressive collectivism – the well-intentioned, but seemingly futile, effort to relieve individuals from economic care by restricting and limiting their power of choice through expert administration by government.

> *[The choice is] between a system where it is the will of a few persons that decides who is to get what, and one where it depends at least partly on the ability and enterprise of the people concerned and partly on unforeseeable circumstances.*[70]

More than a century before Wilson asserted that the theories of Darwin and the new political science would allow government to give us expert administration, the Founders came to the opposite conclusion. The Founders and the People enacted a constitution to prevent collectivism. After more than a century of Americans beating each other up over Woodrow Wilson's academic thought, it's time to move on. In this case, moving on is actually a move back to *liberalism* as Washington and Madison understood it – with *political and economic freedom* as the basis for *liberty.*

Wilson's idea that political freedom could be separated from economic freedom was wrong. And, so was Wilson's idea that a professional group of expert administrators could achieve social

---

[69] *The Road to Serfdom,* F.A. Hayek, supra, at pp 66-67.
[70] *Ibid,* at p. 134.

justice.

Twelve generations of Americans have passed us an economy with ever improving, specialized opportunities. These opportunities rest on the blood, sweat, and tears of millions of Americans.

Consent, cooperation, competition, and chance – under the *Rule of Law*.

Choose your path!

Own it!

Take pride in your choices!

Amicus

10. Who Decides What Is Best?

The most basic question is not what is best, but who shall decide what is best.
Thomas Sowell.

Who plans for whom? Who directs and dominates whom? Who assigns to other people their station in life?[71] These are questions collectivists ask. They are willing to assign the answers to themselves or to "experts" in government – nice, benign administrators, hopefully – but unelected nonetheless.

Thomas Sowell believes these are the wrong questions. *Who decides what is best* is the question. When officials who are temporarily cloaked with the power of government decide for us – the answer cannot be tailored to each of our specific circumstances. Wilson's vision of professional expert administration has failed in our specialized modern economy. Government couldn't catch up in 1912. In the computer age, it is falling further and further behind.

Today, collectivism is inflexible and dogmatic – averse to change – but in love with the identity politics that has captured our political process. Wilson's liberal vision of expert, impartial administration has given way to lethargic, clumsy, partisan dogma from groups – traits unworthy of Wilson's academic roots. The inability of collectivists to walk away from group politics calls into question every label in politics. Who is conservative, liberal, right wing, left wing, reactionary, and forward looking?

Spontaneity, unforeseen results, expecting the unexpected, openness to individual plans, preferences, and interests – these were the Founders principles in support of *individualism*. These ideas are vibrant, exciting, and still attractive in American's 21st century economy.

---

[71] *The Road to Serfdom*, F.A. Hayek, supra, at p. 139

Who decides what is best?

Jefferson chose the individual in 1776. The Founders chose the individual in 1789, and the people of the United States confirmed this choice in conventions ratifying the Constitution in the states. The people of every state that joined the union confirmed the same choice.

This was a momentous decision between 1776 and 1789. The United States turned away from royalty and privilege. The world's first written constitution guaranteeing individual rights was the result.

It is an easy choice today! The computer age is about to be overlapped with the age of genetics. Opportunities for individual Americans to forge their own paths in the 21st century are clear.

A century of failure with collectivism – even though well-intentioned – should fall far behind us in the rear view mirror.

Who decides what is best? You. The Constitution and the American Rule of Law guarantee it.

Valerius

11. Conclusion – America's Road of Freedom

In matters of principle, stand like a rock; in matters of taste, swim with the current. – Thomas Jefferson[72]

The Road of Freedom – the entire package – has already been given to us in the Constitution. The American System of *Consent, Cooperation, Competition, and Chance* has proven itself over and over again. The *American Rule of Law* has protected millions of Americans as they explore, test, assess, fail, and struggle (over and over again) in pursuit of their preferences and interests throughout their life.

Implementation of these principles by fallible people has never been perfect. Black Americans were kept off the Road of Freedom until the Civil War, and hindered thereafter by Jim Crow laws and by prejudice. Women were denied access to many of its benefits under the property, estate, and contract laws of states, and were denied the right to vote until the 20th century. These were fundamental mistakes. Although corrected on paper – there is much more to do in practice – by all Americans -- to make equal access to the Road of Freedom under the Rule of Law a reality.

Individualism has not yet run its course in America. Science and medicine have yet to be conquered. Individuals have not yet discovered an unlimited source of safe energy. Individuals have not yet made vehicles as safe and efficient as they might be. Communications are not as simple and robust are they might be.

We still need things that only *individuals* can reliably produce. Individuals still provide the spontaneity and unforeseen results on which our society relies.

No American should be bashful about protecting and preserving the

---

[72] *Wit and Wisdom of the American Presidents,* supra, at p. 7

inalienable rights Thomas Jefferson announced and the Constitution secured. We have the right to keep them.

> *They who seek nothing but their own just liberty, have always the right to win it.*[73]

Abraham Lincoln's words at his first inauguration in 1861, just after the start of the Civil War, recall the deep connections that have bound Americans together for twelve generations.

> *The mystic chords of memory, stretching from every battlefield and patriot grave to every living heart and hearthstone all over this broad land, will yet swell the chorus of the Union, when again touched, as surely they will be, by the better angels of our nature.*[74]

Our Constitution allows each of us to choose how to meet the opportunities and challenges *chance* sends. *Consent, Cooperation, and Competition* under the Rule of Law is the gift given to every American citizen.

This gift endures, proven by 230 years of experience – *The Road of Freedom.*

Valerius

---

[73] John Milton, *Areopagitica and Other Prose Works*, London: J. M. Dent and Sons, 1927, p. 181.
[74] First Inaugural Address, March 4, 1861.

Bibliography

Robert Pierce Forbes, *The Missouri Compromise and Its Aftermath*: *Slavery and the Meaning of America*, University of North Carolina Press, 2007.

Milton & Rose Friedman, *Free to Choose*, Avon Books, 1979.

Robert Gellately, *Lenin, Stalin, and Hitler*: The Age of Social Catastrophe, Vintage Books, 2008.

Jonah Goldberg, *Liberal Fascism, The Secret History of the American Left from Mussolini to the Politics of Meaning*, Doubleday, 2008.

F.A. Hayek, *The Road to Serfdom*, The Definitive Edition, Edited by Bruce Caldwell, University of Chicago Press, 2007.

F.A. Hayek, *The Fatal Conceit: The Errors of Socialism*, Edited by W.W. Bartley III, University of Chicago Press, 1988.

Friedrich A. Hayek, *Law Legislation and Liberty, Vol. I, Rules and Order*; University of Chicago Press, 1973.

Hamilton, Madison, Jay, *The Federalist Papers*, A Mentor Book, New American Library, 1961.

Oliver Wendell Holmes, *The Common Law*, Harvard University Press, 1963.

Ronald J. Pestritto, *Woodrow Wilson and the Roots of Modern Liberalism*, Rowman & Littlefield Publishers, 2005.

James M. McPherson, *Battle Cry of Freedom: The Civil War Era*, Oxford University Press, 2003.

John B. Miller, Editor, *The Second Bill of Rights and The New Federalist Papers, Eleven Amendment to the United States Constitution and Fifty Papers that Present Them*, The New Federalism, LLC , 2012.

Ronald J. Pestritto, *Woodrow Wilson and the Roots of Modern Liberalism*, Rowman & Littlefield Publishers, 2005.

Ronald J. Pestritto, *Woodrow Wilson: The Essential Political Writings*, Lexington Books, 2005.

Thomas Sowell, *A Conflict of Visions: Ideological Origins of Political Struggles*, Revised Edition, Basic Books, 2007.

Thomas Sowell, *Intellectuals and Society*, Basic Books, 2009.

Thomas Sowell, *The Vision of the Anointed: Self-Congratulation as a Basis for Social Policy*, Basic Books, 1995.

Thomas Sowell, *Wealth, Poverty and Politics*, Basic Books, 2017.

Appendix A Collectivism

It's obvious that we don't know one millionth of one percent about anything.
– Thomas Edison

Collectivism Defined

Collectivism is central direction of economic activity (planning) to serve hoped for social ends.[75] It is government *administration* of parts or all of the economy.[76] For collectivists, the "collective good," as determined through government *planning* or direction, has a higher priority than individual choice.   Individual planning is different. Each of us is a planner, or should be. We want our children to plan. We try to identify, understand, and choose wisely among options, with as much foresight as possible. This is individual foresight, *not collective planning by others for you*. The intentions of collectivists are often good – but not always. When Mussolini began his rule of Italy in the 1920's, the word "totalitarian" was good – admirable because total central planning would be more efficient and effective than the delays and disruptions of individualism. Nationalism was also

---

[75] "It is rarely remembered now that socialism in its beginnings was frankly authoritarian. The French writers who laid the foundation of modern socialism had no doubt that their ideas could be put into practice only by a strong dictatorial government. To them socialism meant an attempt to 'terminate the revolution' by a deliberate reorganization of society on hierarchical lines. . .   Freedom of thought they regarded as the root-evil of nineteenth-century society, and the first of modern planners . . . predicted that those who did not obey his proposed planning boards would be 'treated as cattle.'" *The Road to Serfdom*, F.A. Hayek, supra, at p 76.

[76] Over the past century, the world has seen "central direction" at different levels, from the very broadest national programs, like Wilson's Blue Eagle program, and the five and ten year plans of Nazi Germany, Mussolini's Italy, Stalin's USSR, and Mao's China, to recent, more targeted, but still national programs in the United States like The War on Poverty, the Affordable Care Act, Dodd-Frank, No Child Left Behind, and Race to the Top.

perceived to be a worthy pursuit for Mussolini, the new King of Iraq, and soon, the new Chancellor of Germany – Adolf Hitler.

Today, the aims of collectivism are different – big enough to sweep our constitutional republic away. But the aims of collectivism are not the problem. Americans want equal justice (if not social justice), a good environment, reductions in poverty and drug use, a fair tax system, and religious freedom. It is the methods collectivists advance that are the problem. These methods are common to Marxism, Communism, Socialism, Stalinism, Maoism, Totalitarianism, Fascism, and Hitlerism. The methods are central decision-making backed by the coercive power of government. The methods unite the "ism's" into *collectivism*. Force – coercion – lies at the heart of the disagreement between collectivists and individualists. Coercion can take many forms – the wallet (fees, fines, and taxes), jail, public ridicule, and suppression of speech. In a world of group against group (faction against faction) – every economic or social issue and grievance is a political question.

Marxism; Communism; Socialism; Stalinism; Maoism

Socialism in general has a record of failure so blatant that only an intellectual could ignore or evade it. – Thomas Sowell.

Planned economies have a proven track record of failing. Venezuela (under Chavez and Maduro) is a recent example of a planned economy that led to dictatorship, privation, and private sector collapse. The economic collapse of the Soviet Union ended the Cold War. Cambodia's communist economy collapsed. Mao's PRC and Stalin's Soviet Union killed tens of millions of its citizens through the disastrous economic results of 5-year plan after 5-year plan. Modern China is in the process of trying a different form of central planning – state mercantilism. State sponsored companies compete internationally with the support of central government planning back home. We will soon find out where this form of central planning leads China.

Totalitarianism; Fascism; Hitlerism.

We were the first to assert that the more complicated the forms assumed by

civilization, the more restricted the freedom of the individual must become.
– Benito Mussolini, 1929.[77]

Mussolini was clear about his belief in central direction of the economy for social ends, at the expense of individual freedom. Hitler was equally clear in Germany. There, the rationale for central government control was nationalism. Nazi-ism is collectivism with all traces of individualism removed. The National Socialist party began with central direction of the economy and of education, but the means of socialism – state control – was quickly redirected to turn away from a socialist brand of social justice to Hitler's brand of nationalism.

Woodrow Wilson: American Progressivism

A democratic assembly voting and amending a comprehensive economic plan clause by clause, as it deliberates on an ordinary bill, makes nonsense.
F.A. Hayek [78]

President Woodrow Wilson's academic writings are a principal source of America's brand of collectivism – Progressivism. Between 1910 and 1912, Wilson moved from President of Princeton University to Governor of New Jersey to President of the United States.[79] Before serving as President of Princeton, he was an academic writer in "political science," the new "social science." He thought the scientific method could be applied by administrative experts to solve social problems.

Wilson was no fan of *individualism*. His views on Thomas Jefferson, the Declaration of Independence, the Constitution, and Abraham Lincoln are best illustrated using Wilson's own words.

> *No doubt a great deal of nonsense has been talked about the inalienable rights of the individual, and a great deal that*

---

[77] *The Road to Serfdom*, F.A. Hayek, supra, See Note 1, at page 91.

[78] *Ibid*, at p 106.

[79] Wilson earned 41.8% of the popular vote in the 1912 Presidential Election, defeating incumbent Republican President William H. Taft (23.2%), former Republican President Teddy Roosevelt (27.4%), and Socialist Eugene V. Debs (6.0%). Wilson won the Electoral College.

was mere vague sentiment and pleasing speculation has been put forward as fundamental principle. The rights of man are easy to discourse of . . . but they are infinitely hard to translate into practice. Such theories are never "law."[80]

Jefferson's Declaration of Independence is a practical document for the use of practical men. It is not a thesis for philosophers, but a whip for tyrants; it is not a theory of government but a program of action.[81]

Jefferson was not a thorough American because of the strain of French philosophy that permeated and weakened all of his thought.[82]

The Constitution of the United States had been made under the dominion of the Newtonian Theory. . . The trouble with the theory is that government is not a machine, but a living thing. It falls, not under the theory of the universe, but under the theory of organic life. It is accountable to Darwin, not to Newton.[83]

What commends Mr. Lincoln's studiousness to me is that . . . he did not have any theories at all.[84]

Wilson did not believe individual men and women possess natural or inalienable rights. These were "theories" that could never be "law." The rights of men and women were not fixed like Newton's laws of calculus and physics, and could neither be recognized by the Declaration of Independence nor secured by the Constitution.[85] Instead, these rights evolve and change like Darwin's theory of evolution.

The social sciences were new fields at the end of the 1800's when Wilson was a rising academic in political science. Wilson believed that like the emerging science (biology) of Darwin, the new "social

---

[80] *Woodrow Wilson and the Roots of Modern Liberalism*, supra, at p.47.

[81] *Wit and Wisdom of the American Presidents*, supra, at pp. 44-45 (2009 Rev. Ed.)

[82] *Woodrow Wilson and the Roots of Modern Liberalism*, supra, at p.57.

[83] *Ibid*, at p.119.

[84] *Ibid*, p. 58.

[85] Wilson's statement confirms he didn't understand the scientific method, physics, chemistry, or biology. Newton invented calculus – upon which much of modern science and engineering rests.

sciences" could investigate and then solve social issues through professional *administration* by government officials. But, the social sciences that Wilson and his academic colleagues invented have never followed the logic of actual science (chemistry, biology, physics) or the engineering disciplines.

Political science isn't like chemistry, physics, biology, or mathematics. And, "experiments" in political science don't follow the scientific method of chemistry, physics, biology, or mathematics. The "science-like" results of political "science" have been nothing short of preposterous. People aren't objects to be moved around, managed, and "built" by social science experts. "[Collectivists] are mistaken . . . [w]hen they argue that we must learn to master the forces of society in the same manner in which we have learned to master the forces of nature. This is not only the path to totalitarianism but the path to the destruction of our civilization and a certain way to block future progress."[86]

Wilson saw little difference between socialism and democracy, mere matters of administration.[87]

> *In fundamental theory socialism and democracy are almost if not quite one and the same. They both rest at bottom upon the absolute right of the community to determine its own destiny and that of its members. Limits of wisdom and convenience to the public contract there may be: limits of principle there are, upon strict analysis, none. The difference between democracy and socialism is . . . only a practice difference – a difference of organization and policy, not a difference of primary motive.*

And, Wilson was in the Prussian camp when it came to choosing between *administration* by government professionals and *choice* by individual citizens.

> *If I cannot retain my moral influence over a man except by occasionally knocking him down, if that is the only basis*

[86] *The Road to Serfdom*, F.A. Hayek, supra, at page 212.
[87] *Woodrow Wilson and the Roots of Modern Liberalism*, supra, at 81.

upon which he will respect me, then for the sake of his soul
I have got occasionally to knock him down.[88]

The twentieth century proved the relationship between actual science and social science to be nothing like Wilson's academic hopes. Collectivist leaders of all stripes – right, center, or left – from Lenin, Trotsky, Stalin, Mussolini, and Hitler, to Mao, Khrushchev, Saddam, and Assad – applied collectivist means to centrally plan and coercively administer all kinds of things from the birth rate to entire national economies, with evil results. Although Wilson didn't live to see these evil results, his hope that political science and expert administration would take us to utopia was fantasy.

> *To understand why it is that 'good' men in positions of power will produce evil, while the ordinary man without power but able to engage in voluntary cooperation with his neighbors will produce good, requires analysis and thought, subordinating the emotions to the rational faculty. Surely that is one answer to the perennial mystery of why collectivism, with its demonstrated record of producing tyranny and misery, is so widely regarded as superior to individualism, with its demonstrated record of producing freedom and plenty.*[89]

Wilson had a hopeful academic thought that the minds of men and women must evolve in a positive Darwinian way – like Darwin's "survival of the fittest" theory for species. He didn't see how collectivist central direction and coercion could be redirected by evil, corrupt, or ambitious men to become a direct attack on the political and economic freedom of individuals.

Wilson's progressive fantasy – at the expense of individualism – has not disappeared. American collectivism now takes the form of massive laws and regulations designed to comprehensively deal with social issue after social issue: "Too big to fail," "Comprehensive Immigration Reform," "Affordable Health Care," "The War on Poverty," "The War on Drugs," "Race to the Top," "No Child Left

---

[88] *Wit and Wisdom of the American Presidents*: supra, at p. 42.
[89] 1994 Introduction by Milton Friedman to *The Road to Serfdom*, F.A. Hayek, supra, at p 260.

Behind," "Comprehensive Income Tax Reform."

But, it has been shown that Darwinian theory does NOT in fact apply to government. Government hasn't EVOLVED like Wilson thought, through "survival of the fittest." Rather than fixing social problems, it rearranges, complicates, and obscures them – without practical solutions and at great expense.

> *Collectivism has nothing to put in [individualism's] place .*
> *. . but the demand for obedience and the compulsion of the*
> *individual to do what is collectively decided to be good.*[90]

Atticus

---

[90] *The Road to Serfdom*, F.A. Hayek, supra, at p 217-18.